How Do I Fly?

A Book & Videos for children, adults, and families

based on my daily observations & unfettered imagining

RICH ARMINGTON

2022

PROCEEDS FROM SALES OF 'HOW DO I FLY?' WILL BE DONATED TO:

The Azie Morton Scholarship Fund

@ Huston-Tillotson University in Austin, TX

(Azie's alma mater)

- and -

SOS: Save Our Springs

a non-profit in Austin, TX dedicated to protecting Barton Springs Pool,

the broader Barton Creek Watershed, its springs & streams,

as well as the natural and cultural heritage of the Hill Country region.

Ancestral Wisdom

IMAGE CREDIT: © Austin History Center, Austin Public Library PICA 01009

Barton Springs is a magical land. Well before it became a pool enclosed by two dams containing the cold, crystal-clear water from underground springs, it constantly flowed with life. Comanche and Tonkawa Native Americans dwelt within this ecological community, held in balance by the quiet ways of nature's wisdom.

Even before the arrival of native peoples—and long before it was a human-made pool—the birds and trees, the wind and rains, the fish, turtles, algae, and spring waters brought life. All were welcome.

Yet, segregation is a tragic aspect of the earlier history of Barton Springs Pool. Beginning in the 1920s the city enacted a policy of not selling entrance tickets to Black people.

Thankfully, in the 1960s a young Black woman, Azie Morton, alongside many others stood on the outside and used their imagination to plan ways to swim in the pool that belonged to all. Their creativity, persistence, and love for the springs fueled their courage and sense of fairness. Enthusiastic swim-ins were organized, with Azie and others bypassing the entrance. They flocked together to swim in the pool, as nature intended.

Today, all are once again welcome. The boldness and conviction of Azie as well as many others contributed to the renaming, in 2018, of the street at the southern entrance of Barton Springs Pool. Robert E. Lee Road was changed to Azie Morton Road, in honor of the young woman who went on to become the first Black Treasurer of the United States.

"Nothing has to remain the way it is, if that's not the way a person wants it to be."
—Azie Taylor Morton

The late Honorable Barbara Jordan spoke at Azie Morton's swearing-in ceremony as U.S. Treasurer on September 12, 1977: **"She may not have intended to be an example to others— but became an example."**

IMAGE CREDIT: Heritage Auctions, HA.com

How Do I Fly?

A STORY

Please note: Many chapters have QR Codes at the end that will take you on a journey to one or more short videos that have shaped this story of a family that inspires daily wonder for many at Barton Springs Pool.

Enjoy, and we hope you'll have some fun!

HOW TO SCAN A QR CODE

1

Open the camera app on your device.

2

Point it at the QR code to scan it.

3

Tap the pop-up banner.
Please turn your phone on its side (landscape orientation) for full screen viewing.
[for large screen viewing on your computer
you can type in the specific web address for each chapter]

Why Are They Here at the Pool?

Many of the early morning swimmers know a lot about the birds that visit Barton Springs. The birds were here first, long before people; snowy egrets, great blue herons, grackles, hawks, cormorants, owls, and many others—feeding, resting, and bathing.

But this was different. Two of the most unusual birds anyone had ever seen appeared. No one knew what they were or how they got there. Swimmers sighed in wonder. Every morning the same questions went unanswered, but the fascination and adoration with the birds grew. It seemed unusual and most mysterious that they explored every place at the pool: landing on the water, perching in the trees, flying down the center or across the width of the pool, and strolling in the grass. Always gentle and friendly, these two birds walked or swam politely among the swimmers.

The birds were curious. They were searching. But for what? And who were they?

One day, someone said they knew. They are Egyptian geese. "Where from?" everyone wanted to know. Nobody knows. "How did they get here?" Nobody knows. "Why are they searching everywhere, all day long?" Nobody knows.

And the birds kept arriving, every single morning, to continue their intriguing search.

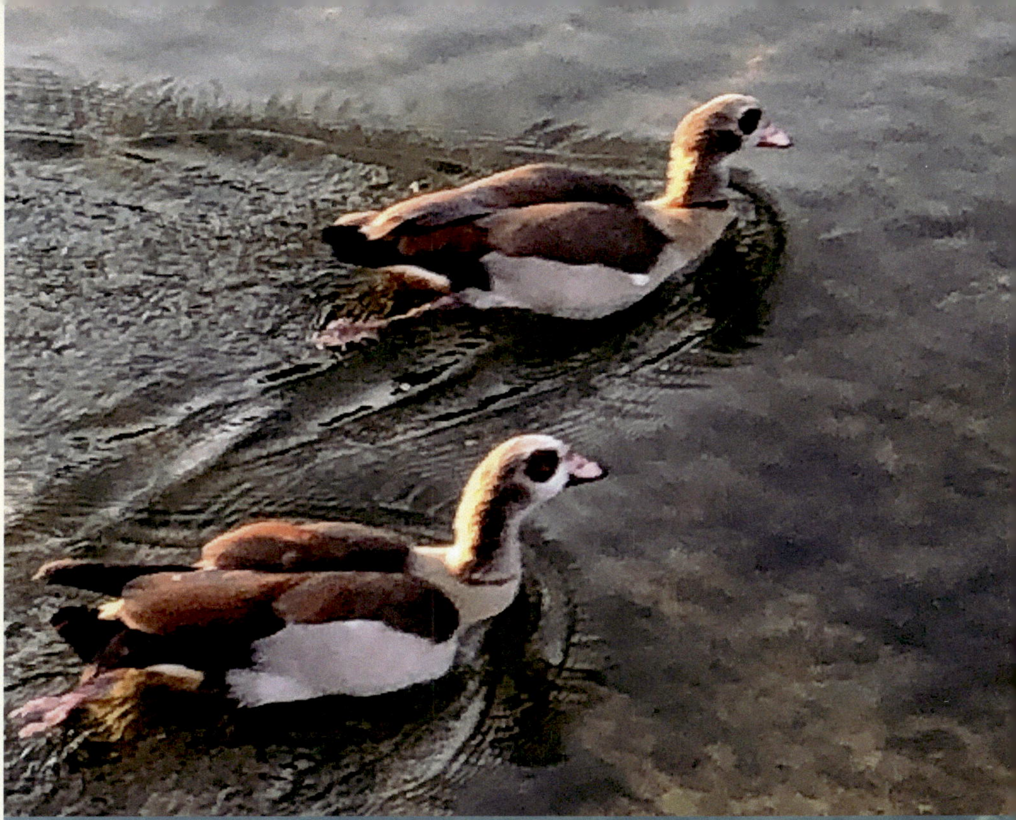

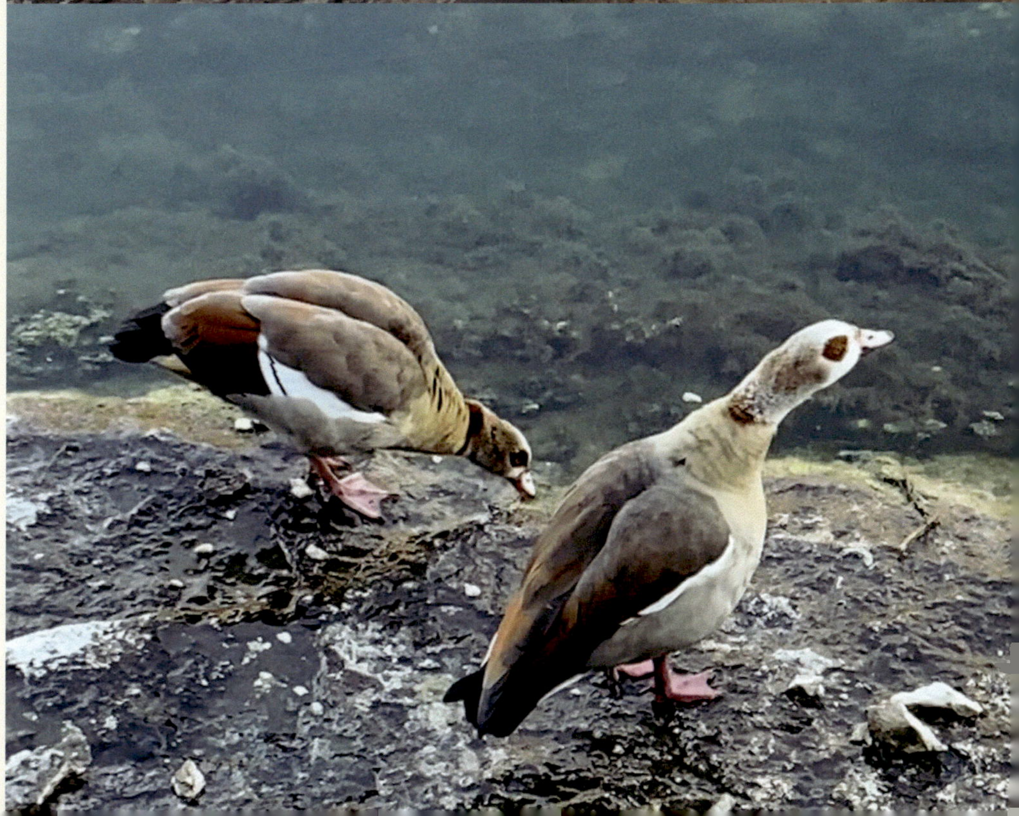

https://howdoifly.com/chapter-1/

Oh No, They're Gone ...

One morning, the unexpected happened. Both of the geese, who had been steadfast companions at the pool, disappeared as mysteriously as they had appeared two months before.

The swimmers were very concerned, they were deeply sad, and their questions continued, though different.

"Did you see the geese today?" No. "Where did they go?" Nobody knows. "Why did they leave?" Nobody knows. "Are they okay?" Everyone hoped and prayed so.

The swimmers kept swimming, but every morning they carefully looked up into the trees and onto the grass hills, yearning for the geese to return and bring back the pure pleasure everyone felt from their graceful presence and waddling ways. Swimmers even missed their thunderous alarm calls when people got too close and scared them.

Yippee! Meet Mama and Baba!

"Hooray! They are back! And look who is with them!! BABIES!"

The parents, Mama and Baba, having safeguarded their nest for two weeks, returned to show off their beauties. They were very proud of these precious little balls of fluff. The babies floated between Mama and Baba, their very protective parents. The human swimmers were ecstatic—and relieved. Some of the swimmers decided they were grandparents. Others referred to the babies as "Fluff Bottoms."

Every morning was now different as the goslings began walking, exploring, eating grass, and, wow, growing bigger by the day. They loved playing together, racing after each other, and were endlessly curious if a sibling found something interesting in the grass. Baba and Mama were always nearby, making sure they were safe. But what was similar was that now everyone at the pool began their day with an early swim.

https://howdoifly.com/chapter-3/

Meet Ruby!

Ruby was the oldest of the baby Egyptian geese. She loved swimming with her whole family, bobbling along with her siblings when they were little puffs of fluff. Her favorite time was when she got to swim alone with Mama and Baba.

One more thing about Ruby became clear: she was extremely curious about the world beyond her family. She loved watching the swimmers and the squirrels. And most special for her was gazing out toward the water, looking upward at the many kinds of birds gliding high and low over the pool. Ruby became even more curious.

https://howdoifly.com/chapter-4/

Scary to Jump Down

Mama and Baba, determined parents, took their babies to the shallow end of the pool very early one morning before it was crowded. It was unclear what they were showing their tiny goslings.

The whole family lined up on the walkway and looked over the edge to the shallow water six—long—feet below. Ruby was scared and held back. She stayed near Mama but watched closely.

Suddenly, Baba jumped. He floated down to the water. Inspired, Ruby took a very deep breath, and jumped too. Down, down she floated through the air toward the water. It seemed like it took a very long time. Mama immediately jumped to be with Ruby. They both landed safely. Then her brothers and sister jumped, tumbling through the air, hoping they would be okay, just like Ruby was.

They were! Everyone landed safely and bounced up and down on the water. Ruby and her siblings had done it! They were relieved and excited. Mama and Baba were proud of every one of them.

Even some of the swimmers cheered them on and talked about how wonderful Baba and Mama were with their babies. The whole goose family had a big celebration by swimming together at the shallow end of the pool and feeding on tasty algae (some of the swimmers referred to the "Family Algae Bar!").

https://howdoifly.com/chapter-5/

Mama, How Do I Fly?

Ruby and her sister and brothers were all getting bigger and stronger. Sometimes they even explored the grass hills by themselves when Mama and Baba were not nearby. It was scary, but exciting.

One day when they were in the marsh, Ruby asked Mama, "I can walk and swim just like you and Baba. But I can't fly like you, Mama. How do I fly?"

Mama looked quietly and lovingly at Ruby for a long time. "Ruby, dear, the most important thing is your imagination."

Ruby didn't understand. "What's imagination, Mama?"

"That's how we make new things, and it's what young ones have the most of: pictures and dreams and ideas that spring up inside you, Ruby. That's imagination."

"Can it help me fly, Mama?"

"Yes, it will take you anywhere."

"I like imagination."

"It's fun. And Ruby, sometimes it takes courage."

Ruby walked back to her siblings. She wasn't sure what Mama meant, but she trusted her because Mama was very smart.

Ruby Gets Toothpick Wings

Ruby's family swam together almost every morning. Mama and Baba knew it would strengthen their babies' legs, and thought bobbing along together would be fun for everyone.

One day, Baba led them up the stairs out of the water to the walkway. Always before, he had led them up the sloping ramp, which was much easier. But that day they hopped up each step for the first time. It was harder, but fun. Ruby was one of the last ones to come onto the walkway.

She realized she was a bit behind and wanted to catch up, so she started running. Suddenly, something very new and surprising happened!!

Ruby felt something move on her back, upward. It wasn't her legs. It wasn't her head or neck. It felt strong and unfamiliar. And it felt good. She ran to Mama and asked her. "Mama, what is it?" "It's your wings, Ruby." "But I can't see them, Mama." "They're tiny toothpick wings, honey." "Will they get bigger?" "Oh yes, Ruby, they'll get really big."

Three weeks later, it was really cold. So, all the babies tucked themselves under Mama to stay warm until the sun grew stronger. Suddenly Ruby popped out, ran to a nearby clearing, and stretched her growing wings high in the air. She wanted everyone to see because she was proud of how large they were becoming.

https://howdoifly.com/chapter-7/

Such Patient Parents!

One day, Mama and Baba were teaching Ruby and her siblings how to climb and jump out of the pool. The little ones tried bravely, but weren't able to climb out. They splashed against the wall.

Mama jumped back into the water behind everyone while Baba stayed out and found an easier ramp. It worked! Ruby and her siblings were able to climb out of the water with help. But then they tried and tried and couldn't find a way to jump up to be with Mama and Baba.

Only a few weeks later the same challenge happened again but this time all of the babies, who were stronger and wiser, climbed out of the water and then jumped gracefully onto the walkway. Mama and Baba were very proud!

https://howdoifly.com/chapter-8/

Mama, How Big Are Your Wings?

Another time, the whole family was swimming together. As they climbed out of the pool, Ruby asked, "Mama, how big are your wings?"

"Come over here, Ruby, so I can show you."

Ruby ran after her mama to a clearing.

Suddenly, Mama opened her wings full and wide.
"Oh Mama, I want mine to be big and beautiful like yours."

"They will be, Ruby."

"Promise, Mama?"

"Yes, Ruby, I promise you."

"Okay, Mama."

As Ruby walked away, she had a picture in her imagination of Mama's wings.

Up-Up-Up! Mama Shows Ruby

A few days later, Ruby was eating quietly, high on the grass hill at the deep end of the pool. Mama walked near her.

In a flash, for no reason that Ruby saw, Mama flew straight upward and landed on a nearby post. She perched there quietly while Ruby stared up at her. Ruby felt so much excitement in her body as she looked up at Mama.

"Mama just flew!" Ruby told her siblings. Everyone was excited about Mama flying.

Later that day, as the family nestled next to each other nice and close, Ruby asked, "Mama, why did you fly up to that post and sit there and look at me?

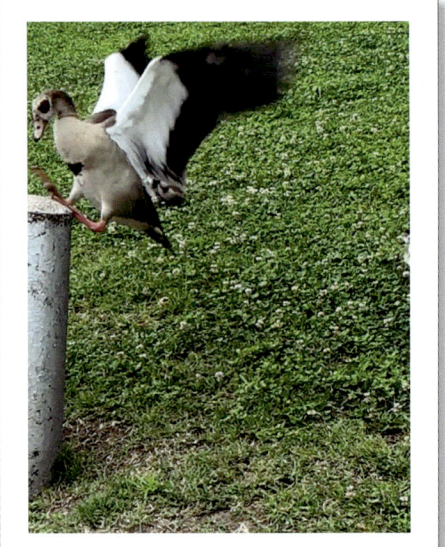

"To show you that you can do it too, Ruby."

"Mama, I'm scared to fly like you and Baba."

"We all get a little scared at first, Ruby. New things can be scary. But that's why you have a family. We're here to help each other."

Ruby liked that.

https://howdoifly.com/chapter-10/

As she took a nap curled up next to her sister, she had a big dream...

Her legs lifted off the ground and her little wings flapped up and down really fast. Ruby was in the air, just like Mama and Baba and all the birds in the sky!

Ruby woke up and told her sister, "Maybe I can fly!"

Baba and Mama Protect the Family

Baba and Mama always protected their young Egyptian geese from anyone or anything that might bother them. The squirrels sometimes got too close to the babies, and Baba and Mama ran at them to scare them away. They never hurt them. Baba and Mama never hurt anyone at the pool, they were gentle as can be. They only made everyone go further away from their babies. Ruby watched and felt safer when Baba and Mama chased the squirrels away. She didn't know about squirrels, even though she thought they were very cute.

One day, a very large white bird got too close to the family and Baba became protective. He ran right at the bird to make it move away, but the bird didn't leave. Suddenly, Mama ran fiercely up the hill. She helped Baba protect their babies by running and flying right at the bird with him. It worked! Together, Baba and Mama scared the big bird away. Then they both ran and flew directly back to their babies to make sure everyone was safe. They were, and everyone continued eating the clover and grass. The large white bird flew away over the pool and did not return. Ruby was learning how Baba and Mama kept everyone safe, and this gave her more confidence.

https://howdoifly.com/chapter-11/

Ruby's Legs and Feet

One day, Ruby was very uneasy. So she ran to Mama to ask her a question.

"Mama, I just saw a bird with yellow feet. Are my legs and feet pretty?" "Yes Ruby, they are just as pretty. All legs and feet are pretty."

"Even squirrels, Mama?" "Oh yes, squirrels' legs and feet—all four of them."

Mama felt protective and said, "Ruby, if anyone ever says your legs and feet aren't as pretty, don't believe them." Ruby was quiet and thought about what Mama said.

Mama waited and then looked directly at her and said, "Promise me, Ruby?"

"Yes, Mama, I promise."

Mama, walked closer to Ruby and said very gently, "Ruby, it's just like all of the leaves here at the pool. They each have special shapes and colors, and they all are beautiful."

Ruby liked what Mama said and walked away to find her siblings, repeating to herself, "Me and squirrels and leaves, ... Me and squirrels and leaves, ... Me and squirrels and leaves."

https://howdoifly.com/chapter-12/

Ruby Naps, Runs to Her Family, and Naps Again

The hill was a special place for Ruby to take a nap. The grass was soft and the sun warmed her back. One day, she woke up and saw her family had moved much further up the hill. Ruby's body felt scared; she didn't want to be that far away from them.

So, she ran up the hill to be with her family again. When she reached them, Ruby's body softened, and she plopped back down on the warm ground and napped some more. Ruby loved being close to her mama and baba, and her sister and brothers. She was also learning that she could do something if she got too far away. And knowing that felt really good.

https://howdoifly.com/chapter-13/

Ruby Red Legs, Ruby Red Legs, Ruby Red Legs

Walking up the grassy hill one day, Ruby saw many unfamiliar birds swarming very close to her. They began squawking at her, and shouted, "Ruby red legs, Ruby red legs, Ruby red legs." They didn't sound nice. And their legs were a different color than Ruby's were.

Ruby was scared. She turned around and saw Mama and Baba were standing right behind her, supporting her, and ready to protect her if she needed them.

Ruby walked a little closer to the birds and said, "My mama has red legs. My baba has red legs." Ruby's voice was shaky, but she remembered what her Mama told her: *Don't believe anyone who says yours aren't as pretty, Ruby.* Ruby imagined her own voice sounding strong, and she continued, "Forever, all my family has red legs. I love my red legs." Ruby paused. And then she said in an even stronger voice, "And my name is Ruby!"

The birds flew away. Ruby walked back to her mama and baba. They told Ruby how strong she had been and how proud they were of her for standing up for herself and their family. Ruby was still shaky, but relieved. She looked down at her legs and felt how strong they were. She thought again, *I love my red legs!*

Ruby went to be with her brothers and sister, and that felt good and safe with Mama nearby watching over them. She remembered Mama's words, *New things can be scary.*

But Ruby Was Still Scared

Later that day, Ruby thought again about all those birds that had squawked at her, and she felt scared. *Suppose it happened again?* She went for a walk to be less scared. She stretched her wings and legs, and walked a long distance in the grass. It worked a bit, but not all the way.

So, she decided to go be with her family and stand next to Baba.

Mama and Baba walked close to Ruby and told her again how brave she had been, even though she was scared. They told her they got scared, too, when they did brave things. Ruby listened closely to Baba and Mama. Then they told her they would watch over and protect her if anyone tried to hurt her.

Ruby could feel their love and protection. She remembered Mama's voice from before, *And Ruby, sometimes it takes courage.*

Now she felt a lot less scared.

Ruby's legs felt strong again.

https://howdoifly.com/chapter-15/

Jump, Float, Swim!

As the days passed, Ruby felt daring again!

She really liked the swimmers at the pool. They smiled at her, called out "Good morning," as she ate nearby, watched her whole family to make sure everyone was healthy and safe, and talked endlessly with each other about how cute the goslings were and how quickly Ruby and her sister and brothers were growing up.

Ruby watched the swimmers, too, as they jumped off the walkway at the pool's edge and landed in the deep water, then paddled with their feet to swim. At the end, the swimmers jumped back out of the water dripping wet, and happier than when they had jumped in. Ruby had never been in the water at the very deep end, but she began imagining what it would be like to go there.

I want to do that, she thought one day. She didn't ask Mama or Baba, though she knew they were watching. Instead she asked her brothers and sister to come with her. Together they walked down the grass slope and jumped onto the walkway.

https://howdoifly.com/chapter-16/

Ruby walked to the edge of the water, but her siblings stopped, hesitant. They were not ready to go further. They looked up at Mama and Baba, who didn't seem worried.

Then, Ruby walked alone to where the water was deep, and suddenly she jumped and glided into the water. She landed and began to bob up and down on top of the deep, cold water—shaky—but also excited.

Ruby's siblings ran along the walkway to keep up with her. They watched very closely to make sure she was safe, and to learn what she was doing so they could do it too when they were ready.

Ruby floated, then paddled, then swam in the water all by herself. Her whole family was watching a little bit nervously, but she also knew that they trusted she could do this.

And she did. Ruby did it!

At the end of her swim, Ruby jumped and flapped up from the water and onto the walkway, just like the swimmers. Her little body was dripping water, all cool and full of happy feelings. Then she jumped from the walkway upward onto the grass hill and ran to her siblings to be together again.

"I did it!" she yelled to her sister and brothers as she ran to them and joined them to snack. They were so excited for Ruby. She also knew how proud Baba and Mama would be of her. As she was running up the hill to be with her siblings, she saw Mama and Baba together up higher on the hill, watching her closely. Yes, Ruby was right—they were as proud as parents could ever be.

Swimmers Try to Fly!

And Ruby's family loved watching the swimmers fly.

Baba's Big Surprise, Fly Away - Come Back!

The next day, Baba walked to the top of the wall and stood alone in the grass at the deep end. He looked out over the water and up at the sky. He was silent, standing tall with his long neck. The family was off to the side, unsure what Baba was doing. Suddenly Baba began to call out with a strong, loud, unfamiliar sound that scared Ruby and her siblings. Mama watched quietly and attentively.

Ruby ran to Mama. "I'm scared Mama, what is Baba doing?" "Trust Baba, Ruby. Just watch him, and keep your eyes on the sky."

So, Ruby did. She stared at Baba and the sky. Suddenly, like the wind, out of nowhere Baba rose straight up into the sky and flew over the water and out of sight.

"Mama, where did Baba go?" Mama's voice was calm and loving. "Keep watching, Ruby. Don't take your eyes off the sky."

She did what Mama said. She looked and looked for her baba. Then, after what seemed to Ruby to be a very long time, Baba soared back to the family. He flew low, right over their heads, and landed in the grass nearby.

Ruby was relieved, curious, and very happy. "Mama, why did Baba leave and then come back?" "So you could see that it's fun and exciting to fly away. And to show you, Ruby, that it's also fun and exciting to fly back home when you're ready."

"Wow, Mama, I want to fly like Baba." Now Ruby also felt excited.

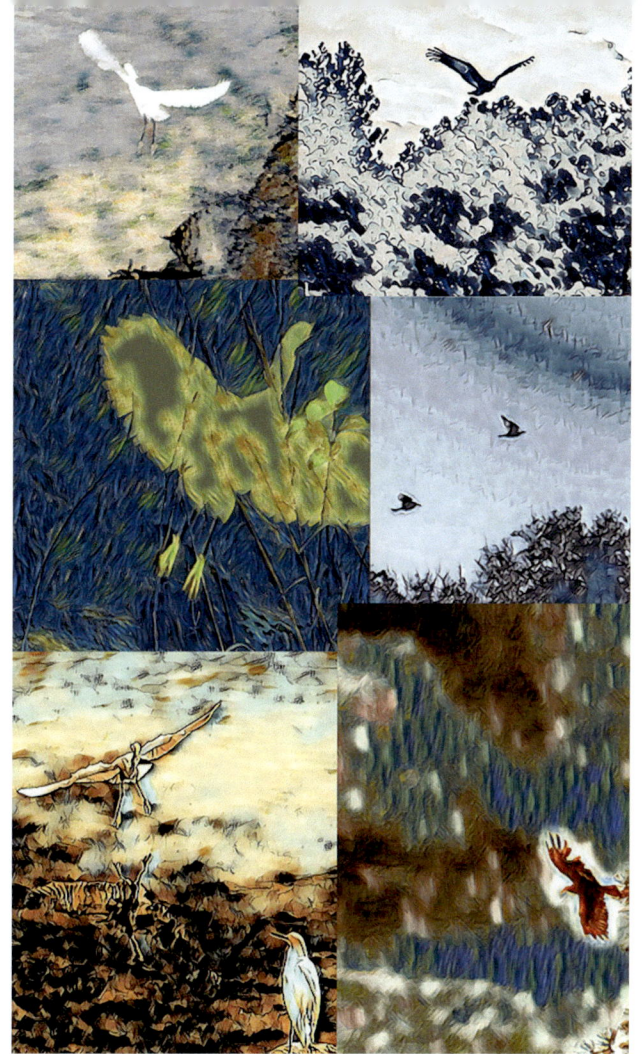

That night Ruby had a whirlwind of dreams....
one after another after another.

https://howdoifly.com/chapter-18/

No Running Ruby - Fly!

That next morning, very early, Ruby left the family nest when it was still dark and walked alone to the shallow end of the pool. She stood in the water, looked up to the sky, thought of all her dreams, and also of watching Baba the day before.

Ruby began speaking quietly but strongly to herself. "I want to fly."

She waited for her family to come to the shallow end, like most mornings. But today was different. Her body felt stronger. Ruby was thinking in a new way. Ruby's family was on the walkway, walking fast, and she got a little behind them.

Ruby began running—fast—on the walkway to catch up with everyone.

In a flash, it happened! Up and up into the air she went, flapping, gliding. Her feet lifted off the walkway, she felt so light. Then Ruby began FLYING! —and giggling—just like in her dreams!

"I did it, I can fly!" she shouted to herself. Her whole body felt light and tingly, and the cool breeze lifted her even higher into the sky.

Ruby landed and ran to Mama. "I did it, Mama, I can fly! I just flew, Mama!"

"Ruby, you FLEW! Oh, you did!" Mama paused... and then asked, "Ruby, how did you fly?"

"I was running to catch up with everyone, Mama, and the sign on the walkway said, 'NO RUNNING'. And I thought, Well, maybe it's okay to fly."

"Oh, my Ruby, what a wonderful imagination you have!"

Ruby's Big Pride!

All day long, Ruby bubbled with joy. She played and danced in the water. "I can fly!" She wanted everyone to know. Her whole family and all the swimmers were proud and excited for her.

A bit later in the day, Ruby walked slowly by herself to the edge of the walkway. She was quiet and thoughtful as she looked out onto the water. Her imagination was active, and her body was full of energy. Ruby had a new idea, a never-before idea, one that made her feel even more alive.

She became serious and began planning, but she told no one.

She went to sleep that night next to her sister and brothers, restless but hopeful, her special plan tucked inside her.

https://howdoifly.com/chapter-20/

The next morning as the sun was still sleeping, Ruby woke up all of her siblings. It was too early for them and they weren't happy, but they really trusted her. Ruby, led by her imagination, walked them to the shallow end of the pool that dark, quiet morning.

"Why did Ruby wake us up?" Nobody knew. "Where are we going?" Nobody knew. "What are we going to do?" Only Ruby knew.

When they arrived in the dark at the shallow end and just stood on the walkway, they wondered what was going to happen. Ruby didn't say anything, she just stood there with them.

Then, out of nowhere, it happened again!

Up went Ruby into the air, and immediately, in a flash, they began running, flapping, and rising into the dark wide sky. Her brothers and sisters flew for the first time, thundering loudly with excitement and pride.

Ruby had everything she ever wanted, ever—to fly—and now—
to fly with her family! YAY!!!

Celebrating Together!

Ruby and her family soared together for the first time, calling out to everyone below. She was delighted when the sun finally shone bright in the sky. Now they could see everything as they flew above the pool. It looked so different from high in the sky—the water, the grass, the trees, the squirrels, and the swimmers below, waving and cheering them for flying! It was even more fun than Ruby had imagined when she was young, when she watched all the other birds flying. Now she had her whole family together in the sky. Everything felt magical.

And Ruby, flying through the air with the sun so bright, was proud of one more thing…Everyone could see their red legs and feet glistening in the sun!

I love my red legs!

The End

https://howdoifly.com/chapter-21/

Some Fun Stuff!

There Are Many, Many Ways to Fly

How do YOU fly?

What can you imagine doing that's new and exciting?

Would you like to use these pages to write or draw what you imagine?

Do you want to put
YOUR family picture here?

There Are Many, Many Ways to Be A Family

Ruby's family is one kind of family, but there are many kinds of families.

Some families have many members or few, tall or short, wide or thin, with one, two, more, or no parents. Some have two mothers, or two fathers, or one of each, or guardians that live close by or farther away, but love is the same, forever.

Some families have members who identify as a She or a They or a He.

Some are this color, some are that color, some are many colors. Your family may not be blood relatives. Some have cute doggies, or kitties or birdies, or hedgehogs, or all of these, or none.

Some are grandparents, friends, teachers, or coaches who love and take care of us. All have ancestors who gave us life and teach us unique ways to fly.

All families try their best to love and create safety.

How does your family love?

Notes From The Author

How Do I Fly? is inspired by Ruby Bridges, the oldest of four children, two brothers and one sister, a pioneering six year old who, with brave innocence alongside family-grown courage and imagination, helped integrate the New Orleans school system in 1960.

Ruby's mother, Lucille Bridges, was unconditionally dedicated to Ruby, her safety, and her education. Day after day, alongside federal marshals, she walked Ruby to school. Hand in hand, they passed screaming and taunting white protesters. Ruby's father lost his job because of her enrollment. Ruby's entire family persevered, however, and the community helped protect their home.

The Problem We All Live With

Lucille Bridges saw this as an opportunity to help all black children.

One of Ruby's most famous supporters was Eleanor Roosevelt, the First Lady of the United States, who wrote her a letter of encouragement.

Ruby never missed a day of school that first year.

"I think my mother and father were the bravest people I know." —Ruby Bridges, 1995

IMAGE CREDIT: © DOJ

In 2011, Ruby met President Barack Obama at the White House. While viewing the Norman Rockwell painting on display in the White House art gallery, he told her, *"I think it's fair to say that if it hadn't been for you guys, I might not be here and we wouldn't be looking at this together."*

My Love for Barton Springs Pool

In the winter of 1978, through happenstance, I alighted at the main entrance of Barton Springs Pool. Having graduated from college in New England earlier that year, I'd bought a worn van and traveled the country with young hope and newfound trepidation. At one point, a hitchhiker, agreeing to share gas costs, passionately beseeched me to drive him to Austin, Texas. For his benefit or mine?

As our first stop, he directed me to this remarkable pool, a gem of this burgeoning city where turtles, salamanders, and fish flourished in crystal-clear spring waters and magnificent trees generously provided pecans for hungry squirrels. I could not have imagined a pool so bountiful—or so welcoming. Swimming within an ecological community I'd never known before, this pool would illuminate my love for the wonder of nature more than mere laps could ever do.

That night, I decided to camp in the parking lot, still without having seen anything of the city beyond this blessing, afraid of leaving this safe harbor. But the police knocked on the side of my van and directed me out of the park. "No parking after 10 pm, and certainly no sleeping overnight." So I left.

But I soon returned. And over many decades in Austin, I have driven, biked, and now walk to the springs. No bad mood withstands the magical transformation as I cross the threshold from hectic urban out there to in there, a natural world embracing anyone and anything needing a place to plant, flourish, and experience buoyancy.

I've developed a daily routine of swimming at the springs in the early morning, preceded by an ancient Chinese movement meditation practice, Wild Goose. I do this on the soft grass hill at the shallow end of the pool near a beloved pecan tree I welcomed as a sapling and have watched become fully mature; it is my steady companion and teacher. My routine is completed by diving into the rewarding spring waters and toweling off while in good-natured conversation with other committed daily swimming buddies. The senses of my day are awakened.

One early morning in January 2021, I was startled by two mated geese standing on and perusing what I thought of as my space, the ground where my practice has been rooted for decades. I gave way. Of course I did. And in time the geese did the same for me, birds and humans sharing the land in gentle partnership.

From the beginning, I was fascinated with these geese—all of us early morning swimmers were— the mates, and later, their babies, too. I learned their ways as best a human with an unquenchable curiosity and an iPhone can. They inspired my admiration, devotion, and yes, imagination. Over the year following their arrival, something in me changed, in slow waves, with each visit.

I fell in love.

This has been surprisingly poignant and life-changing for me, particularly given the difficult events of the past two years: a pandemic that kept me from my wider community; a Texas-wide freeze that left me with no heat or electricity for five days; political groups that infuriate and scare me daily; the death of a beloved family member.

Back to the geese, a family of five babies that one day became a family of four babies due to a hungry hawk. Many things in life left me quite shaken.

But through all this, a time when many of us felt vulnerable and threatened, this silly, gentle family unknowingly provoked my passionate faithfulness.

They kept their vulnerability front and center, their young growing literally while seemingly absorbing a loss and growing their courage. Safety, imagination, and love are required. Mama and Baba showed me the top tier of parenting: just the right amount of protection, the right amount of encouragement, the right amount of being a family that fosters a blossoming individual. This was evident, not in the abstract but in lessons I viewed each beautiful and ever-changing morning.

I can't help but make a connection between the geese and Ruby Bridges and Azie Morton, imagining these young activists also received a blessing of parenting that fostered a broad view of who they could become. They embodied the offering and gave us back hope.

What If...

What if all of the visitors of Barton Springs Pool meant everyone and everything? The people resting, laughing, sharing, smiling, swimming; the trees offering shade and beauty, nuts and leaves for the winter ahead; the green grass offering food, soft bedding, beauty, holding water for the trees; squirrels playing together, jumping and swirling upward; birds of all colors gracing the skies, swooping just above the upstretched arms of swimmers propelling themselves nearby; lifeguards watching intently from their high perches ensuring safety for all; all of the workers keeping the pool and grounds safe, beautiful, and inviting; the turtles, salamanders, and fish hiding in the depths of the water, favored by natural currents as they glide gracefully here and there. Everyone and everything.

What if Azie had it right? That everyone belongs to the pool, not the pool belonging to a few.

What if Azie Morton and Ruby Bridges have shown us that our imagination and our courage are key to fostering a life of fairness, creativity and justice? With the love and support from family, teachers, and the community around us, we can each learn to 'fly' in our own unique and beautiful way.

What if even the changeable, colorful sky, and the clear, sparkling waters are part of this exquisite collaboration of cascading waves of living beings throughout the pool, all dwelling in harmony?

And what if Ruby and her Egyptian geese family expressed the same spirit by taking up residence on this ancestral land with kindness, silliness, gentleness, wisdom, adventure, and possibility?

A Few Fun Facts about Egyptian Geese

Egyptian geese were considered sacred by ancient Egyptians. Appearing in much of their artwork, they believed that the geese were messengers between heaven and earth:

- Family community is very important to Egyptian geese.

- They mate for life and can live for twenty-five years.

- Their voices are normally silent, yet they call loudly and persistently in social situations.

- They chiefly eat bugs, grass, plant leaves, and seeds. They also enjoy wheat, corn, and sweet potatoes.

- Both parents tend to their young from birth to fledging.

- If they are born in an elevated nest, about six hours after hatching the goslings jump down, following encouragement from their parents. Their soft, pliable bodies allow them to bounce on the ground, uninjured.

- Goslings grow quickly, attaining 50 percent of their adult size after the first month and are nearly full grown at two months.

- They often open and close their beaks rapidly when they awaken, a possible sign of yawning.

- Their Austin home at the pool is a good fit for Ruby and her family. Their ancestral lands of Egypt, where the Egyptian geese were revered in ancient times, are located at the same latitude as Austin, Texas, USA.

Special Thanks to Kent Rylander, a retired Texas Tech professor living in Fredericksburg, Texas, who studied the behavior of geese with Konrad Lorenz during the 1980s.

An Abundance of Thanks to:

Heloise Gold, for your sky-high support and quiet modeling of a life of boundless creativity. You have shown me the ways of birds by being one. I've heard your precise calling out to your nearby winged friends, and listened to their return call, a beat-for-beat synchronous response. I'm inspired by the liminal space you all co-create. I've witnessed your magical bird dances spanning more than three decades. This book arises from your graceful, playful, loving, inspiring movement. When you return to ground, your many embodied Taoist sayings inspire us, "She shapes events as they come." I continue to expand from your luminescence.

Steve Finn, for your artful editing, steady generous encouragement, and dedicated friendship. For more than three decades our invigorating discussions, about everything and anything, often result in a fresh and emergent understanding. I'm inspired by our collaborative imagination.

Randall Hill of Hill Creative Group for your calm, perceptive presence, and resulting creative design and layout. I'm thankful for the ways you attended closely to the deeper layers of this project. Realizing you swam at Barton Springs Pool when young sealed the deal.

Robert Faires, for your masterful reading and creative guidance rooted in decades of lively writing about all things art. If postcards could sing—well, this one does—because of you.

Special thanks to the many Ruby Readers who gave this story flight through spirited discernment and essential suggestions. Your wholehearted love for Ruby's family infused this book with a unique lifeforce. Andy Gold, Brenda Bennett, Della Calentine, Donna DeGennaro, Emma Jo Armington, Heloise Gold, Ian Irvin, Kerry Anne Ridley, Kevin Armington, Linda Solomon Scott, Paul Armington, Rick Avery, Robert Faires, الشيماء محمد (Shymaa Mohamed), Steve Moore, Susan Cassano, Toni Westberry, Vicki Totten, Virginia Honig.

Deep gratitude for Hal Richardson, Robert Faires, Tutu, Martha Grenon, Linda Solomon Scott, Elaine Knutson, Nancy McMeans Richey, Yetik Serbest, Bill Bunch, Kalila Homann, Mary Baughman, Elizabeth Garver, Leon Alesi, Beverly Bajema, Cindy Dollar, Marian Schwartz, Cassidy Helikson@BookBaby, Virgie Morton (H-T University), Karen Kocher: LivingSpringsAustin.org, BartonCreekTimeStream.org.

Postscript

On February 17, 2022, as the sun rose, the wheel of life turned yet again as Mama and Baba welcomed eight new babies. Once more, nature's exquisite weaving of vulnerability and bravery offers us the gift of hope. And we accept.

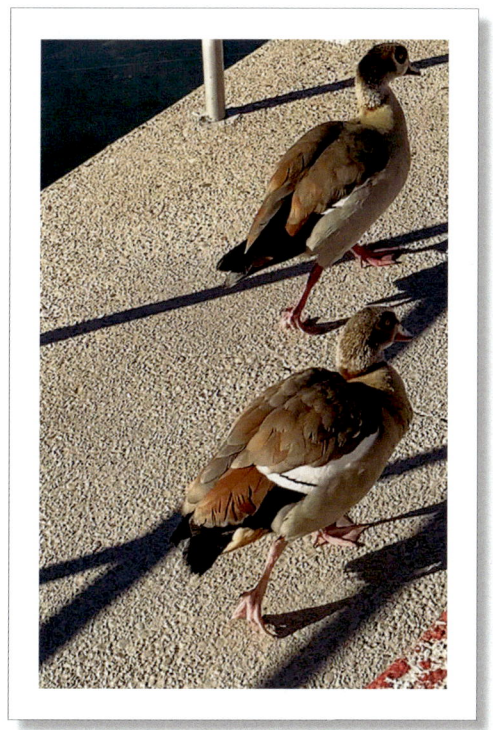

https://howdoifly.com/postscript/

Photos and Videos

PHOTOS AND VIDEOS BY RICH ARMINGTON

ADDITIONAL PHOTOS COURTESY OF:

- Tutu
  [Chapter 1, page 6; Chapter 8, page 20, page 21; Chapter 17, page 39, bottom; Chapter 20, page 44, top left, bottom left; Chapter 21, page 46; page 47, top]
- Martha Grenon
  [Chapter 3, page 10, bottom; Chapter 19, page 42, middle-bottom]
- Linda Scott Solomon
  [Chapter 20, page 45, bottom]
- Andy Gold
  [Part 2: Collage, page 50, center bottom]
- Leon Alesi
  [Part 2: Collage, page 51, top right]
- Lisa Hill
  [Part 2: page 54, lower right]

Thanks to the additional collage photo contributors

ADDITIONAL VIDEOS COURTESY OF:

- Tutu
  [Chapter 8, #1, #2, #3; Chapter 20, #1, #2; Chapter 21, #3, #4]
- Linda Scott Solomon
  [Chapter 20, #3]
- Yetik Serbest
  [Chapter 21, #2]